La pell de brau

Salvador Espriu

La pell de brau

Translated from Catalan by Burton Raffel
Introduction by Lluís Alpera
Afterword by Thomas F. Glick

The Marlboro Press
1987

Originally published in Catalan as *La pell de brau*
Copyright © 1977 by Salvador Espriu

Manufactured in the United States of America

Library of Congress Catalog Card Number 87-81086

Cloth: ISBN 0-910395-27-6
Paper: ISBN 0-910395-28-4

THE MARLBORO PRESS
Post Office Box 157
Marlboro, Vermont 05344

Dedicated, humbly, to the memory of Carles Riba,
because it can perhaps help someone
in that Spain I here call Sfarad.

[Espriu's dedication, 1963]

Because maybe it can help someone,
in that Spain I here call Sfarad.

[Espriu's dedication, 1968]

Prologue to the first edition

After I had handed this book to my publisher friends, a terribly sad thing happened in Spain, a thing of potentially very serious consequences for her spirit and for her culture: the death of Carles Riba. He never saw this poem, and I rather think he would not have liked it: my poetry, on the risky assumption that it was possible, has always gone down roads far, far removed from his, and from those he pointed out. But this is a book open to hope, the hope of honest people and of young people and I should like the name of Maestro Riba—which I must now write, here, in humble tribute — to help clarify and explain the scope and the meaning of our hope, and to help it, through the glorious light of that name, to make itself understood by everyone.

S.E. / Barcelona, August 1959

Prologue to the 1968 edition

I wrote this book ten years ago. Much has happened, since then, many very bad things, and others still worse. We live in times of total confusion and it seems to me indecent, even obscene, to pretend to any kind of optimism. It's said that we're almost at a stage of apocalyptic events: it could very well be—and, of course, it will be even less pleasant if that is what we have to endure. My book reappears, in this very specific reality, in a bilingual edition [Catalan and Spanish]. It's a sign—a small sign, plainly—there are still people who have the courage to take a hopeful stance. I hope many will want to share it, reading how one man, standing on Spain's outer edges, tried to understand, in a backward time, the complex enigma of this peninsula.

Salvador Espriu / Barcelona, 26 March 1968

Contents

Translator's Preface

The "bull-hide"—*la pell de brau*—is Spain's school-book appear-
ance, on cartographic projections. "Sfarad" is my anglicization of
Espriu's "Sepharad," which is, in turn, the Hebrew word for
"Spain." These are, I think, the only absolutely indispensable keys to
the cycle of poems which follows—though there is a fascinating
history both to Catalan poetry and to Espriu's involvement in
philo-Semitism. Professor Lluís Alpera discusses Catalonia, its lan-
guage and history, its literary history, and the poetry of Salvador
Espriu, in his introduction to this volume. Professor Thomas Glick,
in his afterword, sets Espriu's strange and powerful fascination with
Jewish history into its broader context.

I owe large debts to a number of Hispanists. That to Professor
Glick is basic; he first interested me in Espriu, lent me his own copy
of *La pell de brau*, and helped arrange for the granting of translation
rights. Professor Lluís Alpera, himself a Catalan poet, was also
graciously helpful in this same cause. Two of my former colleagues at
the University of Texas, Austin, Professor Rodolfo Cardona, and
Professor Fritz Hensey, patiently and generously went over a number
of these translations with me. Final polishing of the translation was
made much easier, and much more authoritative, by the assistance of
Professor Joseph Gulsoy, of the University of Toronto, a Catalan
lexicographer who freely lent me both his books and his time.

I have worked from Espriu's Catalan, and also from two Spanish
translations, a sensitive rendering by José Agustin Goytisolo (1963)
and the 1968 rendering by Santos Hernandez, the latter with the
collaboration of Carme Serrallonga and Maria-Aurelia Capmany,
and under the supervision of Espriu himself. Curiously, the 1968
translation is not only inferior, as poetry, but, quite surprisingly, a

very great deal less reliable linguistically. Espriu did have a habit of tinkering with his poetry, even after it was in print, but the Catalan text of *La pell de brau* has not been much changed since its first publication, in 1960. (Both the 1963 and the 1968 Spanish translations appear in bilingual editions, Catalan and Spanish *face à face*: Ruodo Ibérico, Paris, put out the 1963 volume, and Editorial Cuadernos, Madrid, put out that of 1968.) The text I have used is that of the 1968 Editorial Cuadernos edition, rather than the very slightly different *Obres Completes* of the same year (Edicions 62, Barcelona). Apart from a handful of extremely minor changes—a single word of essentially identical meaning being substituted for another individual word, or a comma instead of a period—the only substantive alteration is in poem III, and it is a rhythmical rather than a lexical change. Since it represented Espriu's thinking, let me set out this altered version here:

> La pell fa
> de tambor
> percudit
> per les mans
> de la por,
> pel galop
> del cavall
> que no pot
> conquerir
> l'ultim guany
> del repós
> Sepharad
> i la mort,
> cavall flac,
> cavall foll:
> tot sovint
> no destries
> llur nom
> en el somni
> del tomps
> dolorós.

Espriu used many forms—indeed, many styles—and so presents small formal obstacle to twentieth century translation, which is similarly free and far-ranging in its technical resources. This translation is as close, in sense and tone, to Espriu's Catalan as I could reasonably keep it. It is not word-for-word: that is, as I have argued elsewhere, a will-o'-the-wisp of the linguistically ignorant. But it is line-for-line. Espriu was both a very fine and sometimes a very uneven poet; I have tried not to "improve" him.

Espriu's own dedication(s) seem to me so passionately felt that any translator's dedication would be completely out of place. But if a dedication were mine to give, I would inscribe this book to my second daughter, Shifra Simma, whose connection with contemporary Israel is even more substantial than that which Espriu here expresses—since she was born there.

—Burton Raffel

University of Denver
Denver, Colorado

Introduction

Catalan, the language in which *La pell de brau* was originally written, is a Romance Language spoken by seven million people in three countries, covering an area of some 58,500 square kilometers. Deriving its name from the region of Spain where it originated, Catalonia, the Catalan language has survived, indeed flourished, despite forceful persecution at various times throughout its history. Today it is very much alive in the eastern part of the Iberian Peninsula, in the provinces of Gerona, Lérida, Barcelona, Tarragona, Castellón, Valencia, and Alicante, and in the Balearic Isles. A remnant of the domination by Aragon in the fifteenth century, it is still spoken in the Sardinian city of Alguer (Alghero). Catalan is also spoken in Roussillon, the French *département* located in the eastern sector of the Pyrenees, and is, furthermore, the official language of the principality of Andorra.

Originally part of the Carolingian Empire, Catalonia was a focus of Romanesque culture at the very dawning of Western Civilization, around the year 1030. Throughout the Middle Ages, Catalonia actively maintained contact with Occitania and Italy, with Islamic Spain and North Africa. As a result, medieval Catalan culture developed precociously, on a par with that of Italy. The thirteenth century saw the colonization of the Valencian country and of the Balearic Isles by Catalans, with the implantation of their language and culture. At the same time, throughout the Mediterranean area, Catalans were creating a strong commercial and political empire that was liquidated only by the Treaty of Utrecht in 1713. It was also during the thirteenth century that the philosopher Ramon Llull (1233?-1316?) was born and wrote his major works. Curiously, his genius was not internationally recognized until Leibniz signalled his importance six centuries later.

Like the Italian Renaissance courts, those of fifteenth century Catalonia had an entourage of important poets, such as Jordi de Sant Jordi, Ausiás March, and Joan Rois de Corella, and the prose writer Joanot Martorell, author of the renowned chivalrous novel *Tirant lo Blanc*. Castilian writers of the fifteenth and sixteenth centuries found their models and inspiration in the Catalan literature of the period. Indeed, the influence of the Renaissance and the Humanist philosophers entered Spain through Catalonia and from there reached the rest of the Iberian Peninsula. Political union with Castile in 1479 produced a gradual decadence in Catalan letters that was to last three centuries. While the aristocracy and upper bourgeoisie soon adopted the Castilian language, the middle class, the clergy, and the lower classes remained faithful to their mother tongue. For this reason, the one exception to the cultural decadence was in the field of popular literature, songs or poems, often transmitted orally. In the same way Catalan continued to be used in official and administrative matters, in law, and in economic transactions well into the eighteenth century. Beginning in 1707 a French dynasty occupied the Spanish throne. Soon after his arrival, the Bourbon King Philip V promulgated a series of repressive, authoritarian measures against the Catalan language and the political and cultural interests of that region. As a result, the intelligentsia and the ruling class of Catalonia were forced into a subservient position relative to the central government in Madrid. At this point, Catalan was reduced to a language spoken in the home and certain phases of daily life, rarely by the upper class and almost never in official spheres.

The nineteenth and twentieth centuries brought an even greater increase in the use of Castilian, especially in the Valencian region. However, at the same time, the bourgeoisie of Barcelona was striving to restore the cultivated use of Catalan. A group of writers revived the Jocs Florals, a traditionally significant literary contest, in 1859. During the first two decades of the twentieth century, the scholar Pompeu Fabra standardized the Catalan language for use in all levels of life, including the most technical. Under the first home rule administration (Mancomunitat, 1914-1925), Catalan had the support of the autonomous provincial institutions. Furthermore, just before the Spanish Civil War it became the "official" language of Catalonia.

After the war, conditions changed. While the middle class of Catalonia has fought to maintain the use of Catalan, that of Valencia has generally adopted Castilian. Even today the use of Catalan has not been normalized officially. Book publishing has been allowed since 1948. Records have been made in Catalan since 1960; however, the most popular Catalan singer-poet, Raimon, meets with difficulties when he wants to organize a public recital. Magazines in Catalan are slowly developing and gaining in popularity, mainly among conscientious university students and intellectuals. A number of petitions to establish newspapers in Catalan have been presented. Catalan programs in radio and television are almost non-existent, in spite of many requests from the Catalan community.

In the midst of this atmosphere, there have been several noteworthy Catalan writers over the past twenty years: Carles Riba, Pere Quart, Manuel de Pedrolo, Llorenc Villalonga, Joan Fuster, J. V. Foix, to mention a few. They have chosen to maintain their language, often in the face of economic as well as social difficulties. These writers at once respond to and encourage the strong desire of Catalans to use their language in every sphere of life. The trend to restore the use of Catalan, begun in the nineteenth century and later brusquely interrupted by the war, is showing new strength today.

The poet who has most deserved, and usually achieved, recognition both within Spain and abroad is Salvador Espriu. Born in 1913 in Santa Coloma de Farners in the Province of Gerona, Espriu has lived in Barcelona since the age of two. As a youth, he was influenced by the literary gatherings of a group of intellectuals to which his father belonged. One of the results was the publication of his first novel, *El Dr. Rip*, in 1931, when he was only sixteen. A second, *Laia*, came out the following year. Soon noted by critics as a promising young Catalan writer, he went on to publish four more books of prose between 1934 and 1937. As happened to so many Spaniards, Espriu's professional career was cut short by the Civil War. The war broke out after he had won degrees in Law and Ancient History and while he was working toward another in Classics. He did not publish further until the appearance of *Cementiri de Sinera*, a book of poetry, in 1946. Since his prose had become more and more like poetry, the change to this genre was not unexpected. Other works of poetry followed: *Les cançons d'Ariadna* (1949), *Les hores* (1952), *Mrs. Death* (1952), *El caminant i el mur* (1954), *Final del laberint* (1955), *La pell de brau* (1960), *Llibre de Sinera* (1963), *Per al llibre de salms d'aquests vells cecs* (1968), *Fragments. Versots. Intencions. Matisos.* (1968), and *Setmana Santa* (concluded in 1970 but unpublished).

Espriu's poetry of the 1940's and 1950's has been described by one critic as an attempt to compensate, with phantoms of the past, the sense of failure, emptiness, and death that the poet constantly carries with him. Indeed life for Espriu is a grotesque labyrinth inhabited in his poetry by puppet-like beings. He feels that most men, who do not meditate, who do not live with the awareness that they must die and act accordingly, are like puppets dancing about—being moved about by death—in vain. Because of his use of the grotesque, Espriu has been compared to Valle Inclan; yet, it must be noted that he puts this technique at the service of an ethic, using it as a cry for justice and not merely, as does Valle Inclan, as ornament. In spite of the pessimism underlying Espriu's work, the poet maintains the hope that by writing he is serving mankind and that the liberty and justice he calls for will some day be a reality. He says that he wants to give "a bit of help towards living correctly and perhaps towards dying as honest men should." Although his hope for liberty, which can be considered a desire for a truly liberal attitude on the part of all men, is always alive within the poet and his work, it was not until *La pell de brau* that this message was vividly expressed. Published in 1960, this book was immediately hailed not only by younger poets but also by critics as an important contribution to the growing current of civic or political poetry.

La pell de brau is a potent criticism of the poverty, of the intolerance, of the lack of comprehension between opposing views in Spain. Although Espriu's work has obvious political implications, he does not limit himself to lauding past glories or to lamenting the result of the Civil War. Rather, he searches for a peaceful solution to

Spain's problems, a solution that must come from the people themselves as well as from the government. This more positive concern of Espriu's breaks the obsession with death and with the grotesque nothingness of the labyrinths of his previous works. The hope he expresses for the future of his homeland has been called too idealistic; however, one can never doubt his sincerity or his sense of ethics. Indeed, he gives concrete suggestions as to why such conditions persist, and how to better them. The following statements synthesize, perhaps overly so, some of the most tangible messages contained in *La pell de brau*.

Man must earn his freedom by acting honourably: he who behaves vilely deserves the government imposed on him (V). It is necessary to look to the future rather than recall past glories and failures (VIII). Those who let themselves be taken in by cheats merely encourage their existence (X). Since an entire people must never die because of one man, open dialogue between dissenting opinions is imperative. Furthermore, all languages within a country must be accepted and understood (an allusion to the Catalan-Castilian linguistic and cultural conflict) (XLVI). Man must always be willing to work and suffer for his homeland (XLVIII, XLIX). Clearly, at the same time as he deplores the present conditions, Espriu urges the people to earn their freedom and a better way of life, and suggests the means of doing so. Finally, he feels that the hope of Spain is in the hands of youth, untouched by the worst ills of the Civil War (XLI).

The often-used grammar school image of Spain as a stretched bull's hide tacked onto Europe gives Espriu the title of his book. He makes the hide something living, painfully, and calls it Sepharad, the name used by the Jewish people for Spain. By drawing a parallel between the destinies of Spaniards and Jews, Espriu converts the problem of living with one's fellow men—so concretely illustrated by the assasination of the Jews during World War II and by the Spaniards' slaughtering each other in their Civil War—into a universal reality.

La pell de brau should be viewed as a single poem divided into several parts. The continuity is emphasized by the carrying over of an idea or image from the last lines of one poem to the first verses of the next. The first seven poems describe, in metaphysical terms, the historical results of the Spanish Civil War. Here Espriu presents the image of Spain as the bull's hide which the bull himself lifts up on his horns and waves as a bloody banner, representing the suffering of the Spanish people. The inhabitants of Sepharad feel a mixture of love and hate for their homeland, yet they defend their choice. When reminded that theirs is not the best land they could have found, they reply, "In our dreams, yes, it is" (VII). These lines also contain one of the principal themes in *La pell de brau*, already mentioned, that man must look to the future, to his dreams, rather than recall the past or what might have been. Poem VIII again expresses this idea and links the first seven poems to numbers IX-XII which presents various aspects of the degrading conditions of post-war Spain. The poet's irony is biting as he asks: "Don't you know that spigots are designed/ to keep water from flowing?/and houses to keep you/hygienically cold?" (XII).

The following eight poems describe, in grotesque terms, what were probably episodes somehow experienced or witnessed by the poet: the crucifixation of the sun bird, the suicide of the Jewish tailor and the ensuing banquet, and the finding of the three-legged brazier. In XXI there is a return to the high moral tone, to considerations of hope for the future, of the truth and justice that must accompany the destiny of Sepharad. The final poem of this group, XXX, has a distinct reference to the Catalan-speaking populations in contrast to the Castilian: "Men are different, and speech is different/and there are many many names for one unique love." With the appearance of a puppeteer in XXXI, Espriu again presents the phantoms and the symbols—sea, wind, boats—so characteristic of his previous books. The following eight poems betray this tendency. In XLV and XLVI, the poet addresses himself to the strange being present, in diverse forms, throughout his work. Sometimes it has been a blind beggar, or Tiresias, or a powerful being, who can be identified with the God of Job and, in a sense, with the negativist theology of Meister Eckhart and Nicholas of Cusa. In Espriu, however, the divine figure is inaccessible, distant, indifferent, making fun of his creatures even though he fears their rebellion. Also in XLI is a theme repeated later in *Llibre de Sinera*, the hope that youth will save the future of Sepharad: "Only young fingers, but pure ones/Can cure the ulcers in this stretched-out hide."

The final series of poems opens with one of the best known of *La pell de brau*, XLVI. The first lines are a clear criticism: "Sometimes/ One man must die for a people/But never a people/For one man." Espriu then cites the necessity of dialogue as the means toward understanding between various factions. Again there is a definite reference to the Catalan problem: "Your sons' speech and their thoughts, different from your own." The poem closes with the hope that Sepharad can live eternally in peace and liberty. The final poems of the book continue this prophetic, moral tone, at the same time that they reincorporate the symbols of Espriu's previous poetry.

Espriu deservedly occupies a foremost position among the Catalan poets of today. International recognition has also been his: recently portions of his works have been translated by eminent French and Italian publishers, in addition to numerous individual poems and groups of poems that have been translated into various other languages. He successfully incorporates symbolism in a language of civic rebellion, at the same time that he uses the universal themes of life, death, and hopeless memories in a context that transcends the circumstances of Catalonia. His ethical position is expressed through a language stripped of unnecessary trimmings, with every word carefully selected. Espriu's influence is evident in several of the younger Catalan poets, which in itself is encouraging to a poet like myself, who believes that worse times may still come to his homeland and who still harbors the hope that he may help his fellow man through his poetry.

In this English version, Burton Raffel sensitively captures the density of Espriu's thought and the succinct tenseness of his language. Because Espriu's choice of adjectives is so precise—the nouns carry the weight of the poetic expression—the translator's task is difficult. Since Espriu rarely uses two adjectives together, the translator must capture the sense of the descriptive words in as brief an equivalent as possible. This Mr. Raffel has done, giving a clear feeling of the poet's full, taut style. Symbols and images, also basic to Espriu's poetry, are faithfully expressed in this translation. In all, Mr. Raffel will impart to his English readers as complete a sense of Salvador Espriu's poetry as we have yet seen in another language.

—Lluís Alpera

Valencia, 1977

La pell de brau

I

A bull, in a ring in Sfarad,
charges at an unfolded hide
and slowly lifting it high sets it fluttering like a flag—
Yet waving in the wind, this bull-
hide, from a blood-drenched bull,
is only a rag baked hard by the gold
sun, forever surrendered to the martyrdom
of time, our prayer
and also our blasphemy:
victim and executioner, both at once,
and hatred and love, and tears and bitter laughter,
here under the silent, closed eternity of heaven.

II

You
are that unfolded bull-hide,
old Sfarad.
The sun cannot dry,
bull-hide,
all the spilled blood,
all the blood we will spill,
bull-hide.
If I stare at the sea,
if I bury myself in my song,
if I go deep into my dream,
what I dare to see
there in my heart, there in its terror, its fear,
is that unfolded bull-hide,
old Sfarad.

III

A drum: that hide is
a drum
beaten in fear,
for a galloping ride
that can't
ever reach the final victory
of peace.
Sfarad, and death,
a staggering horse, a mad horse:
over and over we lose
its voice
in this sad time's
dream.

IV

A staggering horse, galloping
through dismal years, through the cracked
streets of Sfarad.

Dried-out pain begging for
healing water, for bread.
A thin sprinkle? Then let the bright rain
be water, not our blood.

Our night-time is a listening
ear primed with fear.
We hear fear coming
in that huge bull-hide:
thin-lipped, unsmiling smiles,
a galloping dream of evil
streaming through the streets.

V

If you run
down the night of your hatred,
mad Sfarad, mad wild horse,
whips and swords
will rein you in.

You cannot crown whom you choose—
                    the blood-shedder,
                    the traitor, the rapist,
                        the thief,
or him who never piled brick on slow brick
in a temple
of his own sweat.
The first thing fire burns
is freedom.

Come see yourself
in this thin sheet of ice,
learn the real name
of your disease:
You have studied your face
in the graven image
of this idol
of stone.

VI

Oh idol you've carved for yourself,
portrait of your sickness.

Once, long ago, one day in this our winter,
when this heaven hung low and sullen,
we could see, frightened,
Sfarad's great sin settling into place,
deep in envy's heart:
the infinite sadness of that immortal sin,
a war with no victory,
a war between brothers.
And when we came to the other shore of that sea,
to barren meadows wet, always wet,
with blood,
we escaped in the anguish of our plodding work,
we lit our way by the light of that Temple, still standing
        in our memories;
we struggle, little by little, for the peace
of freedom.

VII

Long, long ago
our grandfathers saw
this same winter
sky, high and dismal,
and read it like a wonderful sign
of protection and peace.
And the oldest of the wanderers
aimed his long walking stick,
sign of his authority,
and jabbed it toward the sky,
marking it for the others,
and then he pointed to these meadows, these fields,
and he said:
>"Truly, after all the endless roads
>of our Wandering, of our Exile,
>we will rest here.
>Here, truly,
>I will be buried."

And one by one
they were all buried in Sfarad,
all those who had come with him,
and his sons, and his grandsons,
from that day to this.
And so we know that we are still
scattered across the earth,
blown by the winds, by the pilgrimage
of our Exile.
And we no longer want to weep
for the Temple,
nor suffer infinite longing
for Jerusalem, our city.

So, when someone

asks us,
sometimes,
in a harsh voice:
>"Why have you stayed
>here in this hard, dry land,
>this land soaked in blood?
>This is surely not
>the best of the lands you came upon
>in the long
>trial
>of your Exile"—
with a small smile
that remembers our fathers
and our grandfathers,
we only say:
>"In our dreams, yes, it is."

VIII

You no longer weep
for the Temple the Romans pulled down.
Your feet hunt in the West
for the free roads of the sea.

Bowmen to the king, your songs
no longer sing from those high
temple walls, preserved,
now, only in memory.

Your eyes see
the roofs of that city.
Dreams come clear, in the dark
knowledge of your eyes.

Beggars born of a race
of noblemen, scattered
by the winds of a thousand thousand
years, we came to Sfarad.

And how we love this new
land of dried crusts,
hard-baked bread filling our ancient lips,
over and over, with the sweet savor of blood!

IX

Sow dust
In this overflowing ground
(Flowing only with blood).

Let bone-weary hands
Tend the furrows:
Dawn-birds
In their first flight.

Let water sprinkle down on Sfarad
In its great drought,
In its famine.

X

If you buy bread and they sell you
Plaster,
Your teeth will crack
As you eat.
Anyone who knew
Flour from lime
Would laugh, seeing
Your tears.
You grow weak, and the thief
Who sells you
Lies
Grows fat.

A prince's servant
Rides by on a prince's
Horse, a prince who walks
Barefooted, now
The servant's club measures
A lost soul's
Head and back,
A soul silent, silent
For as long as its dignity
Lasts.
"Master, how can you stand it?"
"Clown: don't you know
When it's time
To climb down?
It's risky believing
—O it's a deaf man's easy
Deception—that the sick
Old creature's anguished
Truth, anguished, multiple
Truth, somehow never
Throbs, hidden under

Coarse blankets
Soaked in victims'
Blood.
Listen when ice
Speaks to you,
Hope speaks from its chains,
A feeble tock-tick:
But the heart deep in the clock
Never stops."

XI

Time's heart flutters,
Feeble, and leads us through
The two-faced gate
Of pronouns. Sometimes *we*
Is *you*, too, but almost
Never *him*, and always *me*,
And sometimes, over and over, never resting, I say
Jail's first word.
And so we go, linked only
By the cold horror of this stare,
By the emptiness of a few quiet eyes,
Points along a line leading to nothing.
While night's final spigot
Dries away, worn, ruined,
And not a drop of water falls
On Sfarad's parched lips.

XII

Don't you know that spigots are designed
To keep water from flowing?
And houses to keep you
Hygienically cold?
And trains and roads to keep
Everyone wonderfully
Happy, just the way they are
Already?
It never even wants to flow, now,
And certainly there's no such thing as light,
And money buys you
Exactly what you want and also, damn it,
What you need
Except tickets to holiday ballgames
Or that holy of holies, The National Bullfight.
Anyway, while Jehovah and His friends
Fool around with supper, you,
Long-suffering, modest,
Take comfort
In swallowing, one by one,
Big fat words,
The most luscious, the stiffest,
The most enthusiastic words
Served up for you by the newspapers—
Almost without charge.
Ah, what a satisfying soup, what a delight
These letters printed on a frying pan,
Needing no oil, needing no cooking!
And then, glutted, stuffed, your heart
Cleansed, on your long march
Through the pleasant spittle
Of Sfarad's beautifully polished streets,
You fall asleep, thanking God

16

As you think, bravely, oh you creative thinker,
That at least you're one day closer to death.

XIII

We've taken the throbbing night-wind full in the face,
Like some malicious beast lying in ambush,
And waiting for the heavy paw to thud down we stroll in
        shadows
Of shredded fog, to where the street comes to
Its final suburb, and Death opens his junkshop.
It's Miss Ernesta Bacco, not some whore. She comes down from
The Bridge, she rents a room and
Listens to all the door-knobs slowly touched by
Shaking fingers, trembling with time and memories.
There will be pictures, everywhere, bits of paper flowers,
Sticky kitchen smoke, distant steam from a Venetian
Canal, and we'll write letters about the price of
Ravelled mattresses.
Up the stairs—three fat layers of stairs—
We know we'll find the door and the chill
Of that attic-room locked away from air, locked away from
        light,
Where they've thrown nails and cleats and wire—
Forever, maybe—a sad boy's sweaty sweaty
Love, serving-wench purified every Saturday,
She-ass hidden under a child's carnival
Mask, a mask for ticket-selling beauty-queen balls, with
        fractured
Enamelware basins, beaten picture-frames, an old copper stove.

XIV

And we know this treasure, high in a strange
Attic—kingdom of
Cloud-thin space, and cold—
An old copper stove mounted on three legs,
An old crippled stove, green with rust,
And we hoped someone would warm his hands on it,
Slowly—but never stopping—some day,
Here in this miserable winter, here in Sfarad.
And today, while the children's mouths hung open
With hunger, a bony little fish hissed in the pan, a fish
We caught out in the middle of a howling sea-storm.
Three fish, like the three legs on the old copper stove,
And we named them, one by one
—And we wrote it in a fine, small hand—
Justice, and Honesty, and Labor.
And we called the kids to the table, our great-mouthed
Kids, and we made them see the stinking little meal,
So we could soothe their hunger a little,
And then, afterwards, their stiff blue fingers,
Long since opened to the air and the light of that godforsaken
    attic,
Could maybe light up the first, the never-ending, coals in
    that three-legged stove.

XV

Hope is that one
Clear word, that one bright
Word we can use to create a life
Of fire burning in Sfarad's forever-
Returning, fire-smothering winter.

But the dream soon
Wakes up—soon:
We know, we know
The sky-bird
In its cage of frost.

And now the prisoner
Sees his martyrdom
Coming. How we stare at the gleam
Of mountain peaks, in rigid eyes
Dimmed and darkened by death!

XVI

They'd spread the sky-bird's wings
And drag him up the high walls, high, high;
They'd nail him to the wall, rivet him hanging.
His spurs jangled. And after a while
An executioner's fawning fingers leave him
Entombed in a wall, motionless. And then
Eyes staring into the sun's great
Towering palace will go dark, a slow
Humble death. And the imperial
Prisoner will be sacrificed, and horribly,
That prisoner who for centuries ruled
Sfarad's mountain peaks, and its sky, and its dreams,
A homely castrated bird, martyred
To celebrate the end of another year—
Death-anguish of a renegade bat.

XVII

Jew, you who for years
Never thirsted
For a drop of clear water, or
A bit of meat,
Because you'd mastered
Priestly hunger,
Digesting your fast,
Scattering the faint breath
Of sugared brandy, and
Scratching at the ground,
On streets and street-corners,
All over town,
Satisfied to feel
A cold, civil, abundant
Well-being that brought you, completely
Free of charge,
The most wretched gluttons
Anywhere in the city.
When you got to the center of
Town, almost to the center of
Town, a mob suddenly
Shoved you out.
You suffered the sky-
Bird's martyrdom:
Some part of this outrage
Is known, some part has been told.
Fools watched it,
Stiff, frozen—
Not just from hunger
And cold, but from fear too,
Having small courage, being
Bloodless fish.
Jew, observe
This hard, harsh blow, see it,

22

The crashing smash
Of the last wine-
Bottle, cure
For all evil.
How can you drink, if there is no wine?
How can you make it all come out
Even? How can you live, if you can't
Drink? And who will help?
You decide, suddenly,
Watching the sky-
Bird, to fly
With him.
Climb a tree,
Right to the top.
There's a thick rope,
Twelve palm-widths' thick,
Tied right
To the highest branch,
In pious commemoration
Of the holy city.
Put your head in the noose
And let yourself go.
Your body swings, after the leap,
But it soon stops, it soon stops!
We learn everything
From fools' tongues, white
With dust
As they walk
Beside us,
Peaceful people
Who teach us to understand
Blind madmen's
Songs, and their guitars—
Maybe the Jews'
Brothers, Sfarad's old old
Tailors.

XVIII

Maybe this long
Tongue, protruding
In final derision,
Would like more wine?
We'll see.

Under the hanged man's branch, here
In Sfarad, we literate ones
Sit at a table set for supper,
It pleases us to celebrate
As we come together—tinkling our fool's
Gold—a genial little crowd.

The lemon's extensive
Repertoire runs from cask
To mouth. Honey-gold
Eggs hide delicate membranes,
And with words that tell a stammering
Love, we peel their skins.

Observe the night, the indifferent season:
Not a splinter of wind shakes the weathercock.
Our fangs are very sharp.
We let ourselves be gay.
We laugh, one at a time, pleasing by
Excess, the flabby mooing of donkeys and sheep.

We've neatly tangled words' tricky
Rope—what could be easier!
We struggle with the puzzles
Of "evil" and "wealth"—
Delicate minds, oh so subtle,
In which threads keep getting lost.

24

From the lips of a coronary patient
I learn how solitary the soul dies.
I test my body. I feel the relief
Of trans-substantiating myself into a cabbage, or a snail,
Or sometimes a dog with a bone,
After I've rested for a day.

Learned slingshots shoot Reasons
At death—good solid brick-work.
But the wood-beetle and I,
We're hesitant at this criss-crossing
Of alien roads, roads of Yes, roads of No,
And I need to step back a bit.

As always, to smother hunger
We stuff it with smoke.
After our love-feast we put another record
On the machine and break out the cards. I'm never lucky,
My ace gets trumped, the clever one wins,
Gets his money—that's how it goes.

And you want to know
If the whitewash of hope
Lightens the gloomy
Dungeon of a great soul's
Disgust and contempt?
No, no: we can't tell you.

XIX

Don't ask us, you don't know how disgusting it is, weary
Lips pushing in the hole, as the mouth goes on repeating
The words of ultimate coldness, never stopping. We laugh
From fear, hearing the clown tell us
That the soul dies solitary, as alone as a puff of air.
The decrepit wild boar attacks, whipping up the dogs' fangs
As night abandons him, at the foot of this lonely
Tree, stark, bare, where a man hangs, motionless.
Ah, Sfarad! The feeble lights go out, now,
All over, while the great man, the lost great man, puts on
A long terminal performance of anguished notions,
Drowning, little by little, in his wine.

XX

Observe this dead man's mouth: please.
We, the virtuous ones, we examine the livid gaping
Hole compassionately, sensibly.
In minute detail, with precise tact,
We followed all the wrinkles in the corpse's words.
And we said: "You saw how the great fish
Drowned himself in the depths of wine-seas.
Where did it go, the puff of air
That was moving, still, on that strange black rock?
This narrow mountain road, why did it let the withered leaves
And crystal of the supreme lesson come to gay death?"
Light comes down from the mountains,
Enduring light through time's great waterfalls,
And it strangles an implacable hand in its dregs.
Now let's fill the olive-sack and the wheat-sack,
And the heart's sack, and the lips we know are silent,
And take them all to be ground in the mills of Sfarad.
So olives and flour and sadness and pain and work
Can heal sick Sfarad, invalid, beggar king.

XXI

Mills of Sfarad:
Dreams will be converted,
Bit by bit, into reality.

Wind-mill, blood-mill:
We need mills for wheat
So we can have good bread.

Let's go down, using words,
Down to the bottom of horror's well:
Weak words will raise us up
A new clarity.

XXII

For the steps
Of our voices
Heaven becomes, little
By little, a fallen jail,
A shadowy tomb,
And we feel an automatic
Fear of the pit.

Light climbed high on
The tall ladder
Of words,
And was freed:
Day understands
Night's gleam.

But the wings
Watching over this
Sleeping prince—
Ancient steps
Inside a dream dreamed
In some alien time—
They withdraw, moulting
In howling fear,
When we ask them
About Sfarad.

XXIII

We shout from the center of the ring,
A shout like a spear, like a banner.
Under the palm tree the Mother judged
Our people, from off across the sea,
Clear-sighted, clear-sighted, and you said your hand
Would take the rod of new authority
Out of this ancient clay.
Therefore nothing is ever brought to the dry fields,
Therefore we follow roads of cold fear,
Therefore death comes and time goes,
We ask who will become our guide
In this brief moment of the weary marching,
Marching of the generations of Sfarad.

XXIV

If we call you as our guide
For a brief moment
Out of the thousands of years
Of generations walking, walking
On, you separate out gold
And the dream and your name.
Also the hollow
Pomp of words,
The belly's shame,
The shame of rank
Privilege. You'll insist on
Truth
To the edge of the
Grave, you'll need
No one's advice.
You'll never expect
Recognition,
Since you're totally alone,
The humblest of all those
Who only serve.
The helpless
And those who suffer
Will be forever uniquely
Yours—
Except for God
Himself, and He put you
Under
Everyone's feet.

XXV

Let us tell the truth, always,
For the honor of serving, under everyone's feet.

We loathe the swollen bellies, the fat words,
The indecent swagger of money,
Luck's miserably dealt cards,
The gross fumes of rich men's incense.
Our fathers' people are sordid, now, vile,
Crouching in their hate like a dog,
Barking in the distance, almost bearing the rod
And, rolling in dust, travelling down death's roads.

The song we sing in the darkness will frame
High dream-walls, shelter from this snowstorm.
During the night we hear the whispering of many fountains:
Let us begin closing the doors of fear.

XXVI

In the darkness I keep
My door tightly closed
And I keep watchdogs
To calm my fear of thieves.
We hear the wind gnawing
With its restless mouth.

Pages out of ancient dreams
Corrode, one by one.
And fear chews, chews
With quick, hard bites.
Oh Sfarad, our son,
Oh dry tree!

We spin a long silk
Thread for our handkerchief.
But the weavers' fingers
Want the warmth of wool.
From that great sad silence
A free cry is born.
And we wrap this conclusive passion
In hope.

I've built my watchful house
Right in time's heart.
I gave my key
To the light all around it:
Bit by bit the marching night
Turns into dawn.

XXVII

We said: "Oh winter of Sfarad!
We've let darkness rule over us, and ice."
But when summer skies came
We read them and saw no signs of dawn.

If the wind holds back, we hear
The earth's peaceful breath, sleeping through
This hard, hard dream. And now we come out of
Shelter, come out in the open, come out where it's dangerous to be,
And we light
Watch-fires in the night.

XXVIII

Slowly, deliberately we danced in a circle,
Around the fires, in summer's peace,
Hand in hand, chanting war-cries,
Bright light dances from the plains of Sharon.

Who knows earth from ashes?
How can you be free of time, of memory?
High mountains and this delicate ring
Of the sea encircle Sfarad.

You don't intend to wake it from its hard dream,
You stand back, watchful in the cold light.
They see it sleeping, today, and your sight,
Your night, are perfect, oh people of an ancient love.

XXIX

Little by little we forget
And our dances
End, and our songs,
Out of the ancient earth
And sky of the plains
Of Sharon. Because fear creeps into
The beat of our dance,
Fear of wild bears around us.

The circle turns, there is no stopping.
The sun comes out, the sun sets
And there is never anything new
Under its light.
Read
Ecclesiastes
And everything will seem
Easy to understand:
He who wants to deceive himself
Is free to deceive himself.
Now we say "later,"
And later we'll say "tomorrow,"
But we never go astray forever
All in one night.
Men are all different, different,
Thoughts are all different,
We go on living the dream
Of a unique love
And death is quick
To ripen us, death is quick.

XXX

Men are different, and speech is different,
And there are many many names for one unique love.

The delicate old silver decides to stay late
And keeps its light in the fields.
With its thousand perfect-ear traps
The earth has snared the birds singing in the air.

Yes: understand, and take yours, too,
From the olive trees,
The simple, lofty truth of the wind's captive voice:
"Speech is different, and men are different,
And there will be many many names for one unique love."

XXXI

Enter a puppet-master, an
Intermission
For peasants
In the gracious afternoon.
A hat half-hides
The greeting
Of his eyes. But out of the shadows
Rolling
This sad scarecrow
Down the roads,
All harvests
Fail
And bellies of hope
Miscarry.
Chattering,
The songs of the air
Flap like banners
And sweep
All the silver out of
The old forest.
And on this stage
In Sfarad
We hang by threads
Pulled by hidden hands,
Performing the beautiful
Rag-dance.
When the land-wind lies down
Across the fields,
Gusts of sea-wind
Crush down
The fragile painted-paper
Curtain.

XXXII

The wind sweeping in from the sea
Hoots like a prisoner among the ploughed fields.

We watch, far off,
The wind coming and going, the sea coming and going:
We'll sail ships of hope.

Silver trees shift into the distance,
Into the dream of this unmoving time.
And memory dims what has crossed away, over the mountains,
To the impossible East of these years of ours,
By means of the scent of fennel, by means of gardens
Of rockrose shrubs and century-plants, with empty bellies,
Sandy gullies, lazy like lizards.

XXXIII

Up to lizard-waves, snake-waves,
Up to the waves of time's sand.

Burning mouths have drunk,
Nostalgic for water in streaming jugs.

Rain-water in scattered gardens,
Murmur of a fountain now silenced.

The language of thirst keeps
Licking at this mockery, this treacherous belief
That there is moisture deep down in a hell of salt.
The tongue hanging from a salt-stick,
Halfway down the well of our torment,
Stirred the swollen roots of our guilt,
Sank to the bottom of my dry scream.

Like wind trapped in the fields,
We—we, and our clay,
We're prisoners forever in the memory of these years.
In the closed book we read, today:
"Do not weep for death, who is your son,
Except bitterly for him who came down
From far-off skies and from Sfarad's dream,
And for the good earth which will never return."
Good earth of hate, soaked in blood
Which is the fountain of our eternal thirst.

XXXIV

We mock our thirst
With thick, heavy sugar-syrups.
We've confused it, at best,
It was all much clearer, once:
How easy to believe
You know the truth.

Sober, grave, on a harsh
Bishop's throne,
Behind the window-shutter
We saw the wall
Of the peaceful cemetery
Where we will rest.

But can we, one after the other,
Hunt in the sand,
In the middle of a mob,
Dancing this evil back-step,
Breathless, arm in arm
With a gypsy bear?

A beating tambourine
Begins a galloping
Rhythm. And at the edge of laughter
We weep bloody tears.
You never unravelled
The mystery.

Bit by bit the tall
Ships of hope have left
Harbor. Maybe they'll be
Wrecked at sea.
High over the sea
White birds are flying.

XXXVV

Today, white birds pass high overhead, flying south
Through the great light of this huge day.
And little by little they reach prosperous sea-routes,
Clouding over freedom's final ports.
And now fleshless hands play on a tambourine,
And thin lips come to us, saying with hideous love,
"*Haviv*, Spring," and our weary feet
Dance and dance, never stopping,
And we have to laugh, and we laugh till we cry,
Laugh till the consummate anxiety of happiness.
A faint wind blows in the vines, in the cypresses,
Near the yellow fennel, and the sea and the waves
Keep opening out more light, exciting more and more desire
For a high mild sky, Sfarad's new heaven.

XXXVI

We skip along the sand,
Led by the nose:
We hop and jump
With Nicholas the bear.
Thieves and rogues,
Kings in Sfarad,
Dance with us, hand in
Hand, hopping, bowing,
And thrash us
On our backs, on our heads.
Death watches us
From the belltower
In Sinera, crying out
How much it loves me.
Fleshless hands
Mark the compass,
Laughter shakes
This hedge-fence.
Don't say I eat
For nothing, because as I
Drip with dance-sweat
I always see hunger's
Supper atoning, paying,
With broth and dessert.
Black rain-clouds
Soon cover over the
Day's clear brilliance,
And they'll sweep off
The meager harvest
Of these dry fields.
Swallows fly
Grazing gullies and ravines.
Grapes ripen
At the edge of the sea.

XXXVII

Grapes ripen, and now summer's spacious
Calm comes soaring up
Like a wall, and this strange, wonderful
Return sets in on us, eyes turned inward,
And we see distinct lights flowing.
I hold vines, here, and trees, and the sea,
And us, too, under the Sfarad sky.
We fix a final name to everything,
Though old memories come close to shaping a new creation.
You know there's nothing there, except
The quiet, cold, lonely, dark
Light, stairs and whirlpools of light, where words
Go dead and lose themselves in ridges of silence.
Galloping echoes, right to the bottom, galloping
Down the long nocturnal streets of black water,
And we feel ourselves thinking fear, fear, fear.

XXXVIII

It's not right for us to say that name, there
In our fear, his name, who thinks more of us.
If we collide with this strange blindman,
Fumbling in the dark,
And we feel ourselves watched, constantly,
By this blindman's white stare,
Then where, except in emptiness, in nothingness,
Where are we to find foundations for our lives?
We try to build the risky palace
Of our dreams in sand,
And weary, weary we learn this humble lesson,
All down the long length of time,
Because only then are we free to fight
For a final victory over fear.
Listen, Sfarad: men cannot exist
Not free.
When will Sfarad understand that we cannot exist
Not free.
And the people cry, in one voice, "Amen."

XXXIX

Because eyes submitted to the sadness of waiting,
And the seven-branched candelabrum
Burned a long time,
Perhaps we can tell ourselves that night has flickered down.
We know, now, that the stars will be
Put to work for the grandeur of humanity:
These are new words, pronounced by the mouth
Out of death's final mocking smile.
Then man will be free,
And happy, even in Sfarad.
But we felt ourselves alone
In front of the window, in front of the blindman's
Little white daughters, the strange fortune-teller,
And we did not forget what the ancient law commanded:
"Thou shalt not lie, nor steal, nor kill . . ."
Eternal rules
Valid everywhere, in Israel and in the Exile of the Jews,
In that Kingdom almost conquered by the stars
And also, some day, in Sfarad.
At least, on Sfarad's Day
Of Judgment.

XL

But you're kidding yourself:
You think spiders
Always have thread.

You want me to be
A leper and you'll let me
Be covered with dung.

And you sell
The drapers, free, cloth
Cut from the bull-hide.

Fool: are you anxious
To gnaw our bones
Down to the very marrow?

We'll show this glutton
All the skeletons'
Old cheeks.

You burst, filled to the brim,
And we grow
Leaner and leaner.

See the hired soldiers
Cutting hay for their horses,
Deep in airy meadows.

Wrapped in smoke,
You close your eyes
And can't see the world.

But when you do wake up,
Oh the laugh on your lips
Will slow you down.

XLI

You laugh with us, with those
Who dream, always, with open eyes.
But when you look deep into the mirror, you're afraid
Of those who know how to sleep with their eyes open.

A leper, naked in the ashes.
Three kind friends, and later another one too,
Weep with happiness over his unhappiness.
And his voice never dripped with the dust of ages:
"Can you tell me if Man is more just, or God?"

I came closer to the spider, bit by bit,
He crawls to the empty well, moving heavily.
You die of striped-hooves, noiseless,
Air, glass, life, prison-time.
I can read a name in the dark stones.
Even if he throws me down, what a pillow death is!

Running down thirst's long rope,
Down sad poetry's parched dryness,
With a cup of heaven's bright charity.
The wings of angelic falcons beat at me,
Word-swords chop at my legs.
But the water saved for my wasteland,
The anxiety of hope, on burning lips.

His cowardly appetite, the returning son,
Falling on his face among the leavings pigs won't eat.
His father throws him stones of forgiveness,
Sops of doctrine with crumbs of words.
The prodigal begins to wail the softest of wails:
If you're hungry, try to pretend that you're good.

Guided by the blindest of all, the blindmen proceed
Toward the abysses of cruelty.
How shall we stop these hesitant marchers,
When they think themselves free to understand evil
With the calm whiteness of an unmoving stare?
While they shriek with fear
A new row of them walks carefully
Into the eternal darkness which will swallow them down.

Rich old one, lonely, having no heir,
You hunt in vain for a bit of advice
About adding to your piled-up dry mountains of gold.
You'll buy no rest on your eternal bed.
The dawn of that gold-night will never come,
You'll never be able to learn the lesson of that cry:
"Oh God of Israel!
Only young fingers, but pure ones,
Can cure the ulcers in this stretched-out hide."

XLII

May those young hands
—Cold, strong, pure—
Know how to count!

You're the heir
Of days of hate
And misrule.

Watch carefully
Where the pot of gold
Is hidden.

If you love power
It can be yours,
And then you can lead.

We go down into the abyss
On ropes of light
Spun in deep dreams.

Shipwrecked boats
Sail sweetly
Out to sea.

Let your eyes
Climb out of the abyss,
Blindmen, on stairways of smoke.

It's a short life, flower:
The anxieties of hope,
Sorrow's slow boring labor.

I soothed my thirst,
And hell laughed
Charitably.

The prince of the world
Sat at our table,
Along with Death.

We glutted ourselves on the loins
And ribs of other
Honorable hogs.

And then, slobbering nicely,
We quickly
Rose from the table.

Our teeth all got to
The same marrow
Of great and glorious ideas.

Grindstones smashed
The strong spines
Which had so humbled themselves.

Soul. Only
A bit of air
Blown in by the wind?

Questions. Names
Are stones thrown
By strange slingshots.

They turn against you.
They bury you, great heavy
Ruined castles.

We take numbers
Down dirt paths
As far as Unity.

And our courage has deserted,
Leaving us with
No flock, no shepherd.

Not knowing why,
The hollow nothingness
Hides words.

We draw the arrow
Of our mourning
From time's quiver.

And out of the cry
A dagger strikes at
Sfarad's hard heart.

XLIII

—Mourning hunts me in the dry land,
In the leaden steps of lost time.
But it leaves no sign
In gallows-meat, in hospital-flesh.

—In the stomach, only the blow of
The squeamish one's song:
Nothing else comes out of the wall
To this heart of a world with no future.

—Wheat doesn't grow in corn-fields,
And anyway it never rains in Sfarad.
Let the fields rot, the earth is bone-dry.
Let's look up, let's see the sun.

XLIV

Blue
Against the sun
This trunk
Of a dead tree.
Broad falcon
Wings
Over stubble
Fires.
Nothing ripe
In furrows,
No whisper
Of new wind
In reeds.
No song-
Joy, no song-
Relief.
Dust, dust, dust
Of sluggish sheep
In the harvest's
Heart.
And in the fear
That I am,
That all of us
Are, only
Memory opens
For dried-out
Dust and yearning
For ancient ice
In fountains,
The road
Of never ever
Returning.

XLV

We go back through memory to ancient steps
Walking this road. But we see
No new fountain, no sign of water,
In happiness' well.

Sky of crows. Inexorable
Screaming song across the wasteland:
"If one man dies for his people,
Our people die for nothing."

XLVI

Sometimes
One man must die for a people,
But never a people
For one man:
Always remember this, Sfarad.
Let dialogue follow freely from point to point
And try to understand, to appreciate
Your sons' speech and their thoughts, different from your own.
Let rain fall in the fields, little by little,
And let the air move like an extended hand,
Gentle and kind, over the broad fields.
Let Sfarad live for all eternity
In order, in peace, in labor,
In noble and difficult
Freedom.

XLVII

In the law and in the covenant
Which you will keep forever,
In the steadiness of your dialogue
With your equals,
Build the slow temple
Of your labor,
Raise your new house
On ground
Which you will name
Freedom.

And you, man of today, of now
In Sfarad,
No longer live the death
Of cowardly peace,
Let it go, save yourself
From your evil.
Sail on stormy seas,
Light your way with bright lightning.
Far from this safe harbor,
Wash away
All the blood
Of this trampled-down
Bull-hide
In the waters of hope.

XLVIII

Live, and you won't have wanted to feel in danger:
How urgently fear signals you,
Along the road running from a free sea
To death's safe shore.
You've said "life," you've said "risk,"
And you've said the same thing with two useless words.
Don't still listen to the three-headed dog
Howling, and to night's songs, and to laughing eunuchs
Who want you never to be
Who you are—only you, one single
Man, with no other name—you and your truth.
Think, work, fight, and suffer for Sfarad,
Under the rain and under the snow, in the gay lightning-sea.
And then you'll always have time to run from danger
And steer or row to the sadness of harbors.

XLIX

Leave eunuchs' blubbering, their fluttering with sterile laughter,
And when they bore you, stop them with a closed fist.
You'll be a man, then, not an old witch afraid of her shadow,
And you'll find no loftier dignity, never and
Nowhere in this world whose eyes watch and understand.
What can drag you down, what evil can you fail to endure,
If you accept time and death and the honor of serving,
Noble commandments of the eternal law?
Contemptuous of flattery, of profits and rewards,
Work hard to make Sfarad forever
Proud, never a trembling slave.
And when you come to the door of your own night,
At the end of that road from which no return is possible,
You'll know how to say, for yourself, "My thanks for
        having lived."

L

Sailing straight through danger,
When your eyes have learned to decipher
The sea's great calm secret, deep
Inside snowstorms, and we clear the way
For the ship to sail the final dangerous waters,
Perhaps you'll no longer feel sadness
Pursuing the peaceful
Port of our return,
On the edge of night.
And then, loving the earth, we'll come
Through the dust to that tree which
Grows forever out of the
Heart of all things,
And there our road will end.

LI

We've walked, and today we rest
In the generous peace of that tree,
Sheltered against the great wind at the edge of night.
We've loved the earth and
We've loved our dream of a new home
Built on free soil.
Not a safe flower, no, but we've plucked
The hope of safe flowers, and we've carried it
All along this dust of journeys.
And now we cast away words
And we feel ourselves come to silence,
Through the soft sound of a distant galloping.

LII

In this silence
Surrounded by empty noise,
A broad bull-hide
That everyone tramps on.
When young fingers
Raise it from the dust
It will tremble, on high,
In the tranquillity
Of those who loved it as a
Bloody rag,
Of those who served it
Through days of sadness.

That distant procession
Is close, now, very close.
First comes
An ambling horse.
A faceless trooper
Laughs our name.
We hear the cold word
Unafraid,
Since hope saves for us
That ultimate pure
Naked heart, stripped
Of men, of that well
From which hatred grows, and
All the great pain
Of that ancient evil which is drowned
By the waters of forgiveness.

LIII

With the unique reward of our
Modest hope, when the procession
Comes down through the night we'll be
Free, we'll no longer walk like
Or be ruled by the feeble shambler.

Because all that huge number of words
Studied and arranged in good order
Will sink slowly into silence, and be lost,
And all we'll want to write, now,
Is your name.

LIV

All we
Want,
Humbly
Hopeful,
Is the eternal abundance
Of the rose,
A supreme eternity
Of flowering.

While the houses of the night
Shut down, one by one,
And darkness pierces
Through to dawn's
Fountains,   -
The blindman's
Perceptive fingers
Teach our eyes
To see and to know,
To understand
With slow love.

Thus we've surveyed
Rivers and mountains,
Dry highlands and cities,
And we've dreamed every dream
Men dream.
We've been with the wind
In fields and in woods,
In the whispering of leaves and fountains,
And we go on writing, here

On this stretched-out hide,
And in a secret, immortal heart,
Bit by slow bit, the name
Sfarad.

Lavinia, June 1957.
Sinera, July 1958.

Afterword
Catalans as Jews: Catalan Philosemitism in the Franco Era

When I first travelled in Catalonia in the mid-1950s I was unaware of the Catalan language and its flourishing literature. Like many Americans, I passed through Barcelona, culturally incurious, interested only in the monuments and shops. I was unaware, too, of any particular kinship between Catalans and Jews; nor could I then have comprehended how any Spaniard, looking inward, could find Sepharad, and not Spain.

Returning to Barcelona in the fall of 1960 to begin a year of study in the Department of Semitic Languages at the University, I embarked at the same time upon a discovery of Catalan culture, my devotion to which steadily deepened, in part as a response to a completely unexpected environment of philosemitism. I was made to feel that I had, in a real sense, come home; but why this should be remained a mystery to me for a long time.

My initial and immediate circle of friends was composed of my fellow semitic scholars, but, given the equal emphasis in the department on Hebrew and Arabic, on Jewish and Islamic studies, I would not have been surprised had my classmates reflected the pro-Arab orientation of the Franco regime and mass-media. These companions of mine were by no means non-conformist, either politically or intellectually, but rather from conservative, middle class families, and many of the group were extremely observant Catholics, who went to Mass daily. (The Catalans among them were nationalists and one later ran for senator on a conservative ticket in the late 1970s.) Yet it would be a distinct understatement to say that my friends' attitudes toward Jews and Jewish culture exceeded mere tolerance. The group's general knowledge of Israeli culture was superior to my own—they danced the hora, sang Hebrew songs, and three of the women have since spent extended periods in Israel, living and working on kibbutzim.

To a certain extent this group reflected the values of the department's chief figure at the time, the late hebraist Josep M. Millàs i Vallicrosa, a devout Catholic who spoke rapid-fire Hebrew with a thick Catalan accent.[1] Millàs himself had been the first visiting professor at Hebrew University in the late 1930s where he went to escape the trials of the Spanish Civil War. (As a conservative he could not favor the Republic, nor, as a Catalan nationalist, the insurgents.) Millàs never let his admitted philosemitism interfere with his interpretation of Biblical texts: for this great hebraist, the Catholic exegetical tradition was right and the Jewish one wrong, whenever the two were in conflict. I will never forget his horror when Mair José Benardete asserted at a public lecture in Barcelona that the Song of Songs was a poem about physical love. Philosemitism bore different ideological charges for conservatives and progressives in this period, although Catalan nationalism was a unifying undercurrent.

Five years later in Valencia I found a new group of philosemites, of radically different character from my Barcelona friends. These Valencians were all pan-Catalan nationalists, socialist, non-observant when not atheist, and without any contact whatever with Jews. Yet they had the same Hebrew phonograph records, the same books about Israel, and the same interest in kibbutzim and the Israeli social and economic experience as the Barcelona group.

But while this discovery was gratifying, I was no longer surprised at finding philosemitic attitudes in the Catalan-speaking regions of Spain. Since 1960 I had been making mental notes about the scope and background of Catalan philosemitism, some of which I present here as a revealing and little appreciated facet of contemporary Catalan culture.

For a decade encompassing most of the 1960s, there was a steady flow of translation of books of Jewish interest into the Catalan language (all published in Barcelona, the hub of Catalan intellectual life). Among the most significant of these were the novelist Ramon Folch i Camarasa's translation of Anne Frank's diary (*Diari*, Editorial Selecta, 1959), the poet Joan Oliver's translation of Schwarz-

Bart's *The Last of the Just* (*El darrer just*, Editorial Vergara, 1963) and Domènec Guansé's selection of the poetry of Nelly Sachs (*La passió d'Israel*, Ediciones Grijalbo, 1967).

Works of a more popular nature, such as Leon Uris's *Exodus* (*Exode*, translated by Marçal Trilla i Rostoll, Editorial Mateu, 1965) have also enjoyed wide distribution. (The Castilian version of *Exodus*, also published in Barcelona, as are many other Castilian translations of Jewish works, was extremely popular throughout Spain; it went through nineteen printings between March 1960 and June 1963.) There also appeared non-fiction works about Israel, including André Chouraqui's *L'Estat d'Israel* (translated from the French, Edicions 62, 1963), with a prologue by the social historian Josep Benet, and also a translation of the special number of *Les Temps Modernes* dedicated to Arab-Israeli dialogue (*El conflicte àrab-israelita*, Edició de Materials, 1967). In addition, the magazine of the Abbey of Montserrat, *Serra d'Or*, the only monthly which the Franco regime allowed to be published in Catalan and still one of the most serious and respected journals in Spain, has printed frequent articles on Israeli topics, though more in the 1960s than in succeeding years.

The interest of the publishers reflected the double focus of Catalan philosemitism: the Nazi persecution and the renaissance of the Jewish state. It is important to understand the rationale of this two-sided approach, for its roots are completely internal to Catalan culture and are not to be explained by any vital contact with Jews, for there has been none, but only by the Catalan political and cultural experience of the past century. (Of course, there is a Jewish community of several thousands in Barcelona, but it is composed of recent immigrants, is Castilian-speaking, business-oriented, and has few links with the Catalan intellectual community.)

The first pole of Catalan attraction to Jews is admiration and sympathy for the deliberate and ideologically coherent rebirth of a moribund national culture, the history of whose reconstruction closely parallels Catalonia's own experience. A comparative study of Jewish and Catalan nationalism and cultural revival in the past 150 years would reveal striking similarities, not only in internal development (specifically the relationship between nationalism and linguistic revival), but also in the position of the cultural minority relative to the alien groups which surround and dominate it.

The Catalan language which in the middle ages had been the vehicle of a great literature (the chivalresque novel *Tirant lo Blanc* by the medieval Valencian author Joanot Martorell is the work best known in the United States today) entered upon a period of decline from the time of the merger of the crowns of Aragon and Castile in the late fifteenth century.[2] Although Catalan continued to be spoken in the home throughout the Catalan provinces, the Balearic Islands, and the littoral areas of the Kingdom of Valencia, and lingered on for a while in local administrative use, Catalans grew more and more accustomed to writing in Castilian, the official language of united Spain which had behind it all of the institutional and educational supports which Catalan now lacked.

The Enlightenment largely passed Catalonia by, and the Catalans who participated in the advances of that epoch usually expressed themselves in Castilian. (The one exception, interestingly enough, was the island of Menorca—then under British rule—which enjoyed a moment of cultural revival at the end of the eighteenth century whose literary and scholarly works were realized in the Catalan language.) Cultural decay was well-advanced until the mid-nineteenth century when a vast movement of cultural renaissance—*la Renaixença*—took hold in Catalonia, drawing support and momentum from the political and economic interests of the flourishing industrial bourgeoisie of Barcelona who were desirous of asserting their independence from Madrid.

The political culmination of this movement was the statute of autonomy granted the four Catalan provinces by the Second Republic (September 1932), which gave the Catalans the political and cultural autonomy they had been seeking since the nineteenth century. More importantly, Catalan had become again a living language of literary and intellectual expression, matching Castilian production in poetry, fiction and scholarship. Broad similarities with recent Jewish history are quite obvious in the foregoing capsule history. The Renaixença and the movement for political autonomy closely parallel, both chronologically and thematically, the *Haskalah* and the development of Zionist ideology and programs.

In September 1960, *Serra d'Or* published an abridgement of an essay by Chaim Rabin on the rebirth of Hebrew.[3] The article was printed without comment and contained no allusions to the Catalan situation. But the associations suggested by the rubrics of the discussion could not have been lost on any Catalan reader. Both languages, Hebrew and Catalan, had a classical period in the relatively distant past, after which linguistic development was sharply curtailed. Catalan declined as a literary language, although daily speech continued; the Hebrew case was just the reverse. Then in a period of renaissance occurring contemporaneously in both cultures the language was revived as an instrument of modern literary expression and as a rallying point for nationalism: the central and eastern European Haskalah and the Catalan Renaixença.

The institutions and processes of linguistic revival as well as the problems encountered in modernizing a language were also strikingly similar in both cases. In the formulation of modern grammatical and orthographical rules, the Catalan grammarian and lexicographer, Pompeu Fabra (1868-1948), played a role analogous to that of Eliezer ben Yehuda (1858-1923). Both were authors of monumental dictionaries and both, in turn, became symbols of linguistic revival.

The problems facing both Catalan and Hebrew in the twentieth century are obviously similar. The revived language has to be made adaptive to new concepts lacking in the classical lexicon, especially in the areas of science and technology. To this end both cultures established similar institutions to oversee the invention and standardization of neologisms (the Vaad ha-Lashon and the philological section of the Institut d'Estudis Catalans). The Israeli efforts in modernization are well-publicized, in publications of the Technion, for example, while *Serra d'Or* publishes periodic lists of "additions to the dictionary," in the same way that Hebrew neologisms are circulated by the mass media in Israel. Finally, the Rabin article discussed the mechanisms of language training for immigrants, suggesting broader problems of acculturation and social adjustment of particular and immediate interest to Catalans. The *ulpan* could only have been regarded as a felicitous, if not enviable, model by Catalan intellectuals preoccupied with the catalanization of Castilian-speaking immigrants who in the course of the century had immigrated from Murcia and Andalusia, seeking work in the factories of Barcelona.

The theme of education and cultural initiation of the young in the face of a surrounding alien majority is an obvious attraction of another recent translation: Lena Pougatch-Zalcman's memoirs of the famous Hebrew nursery school of pre-War Vilna (*Els infants de Vilna*, Editorial Nova Terra, 1971). The *gan* of Vilna was a school where Lithuanian Jewish children could begin education in a Hebrew environment completely distinct from the surrounding gentile culture. Aside from its pedagogical interest, it is clear that the Vilna experience set a poignant example for the Catalan reader of the late Franco period. The education of children to norms of Catalan language and literature was still a precarious enterprise, at a time when official Castilian dominated the state schools and instructional norms were handed down from Madrid. Moreover, the on-going immigration of Castilian speakers into Catalonia ensured the continuation of a precarious balance between the desire for a strongly Catalan culture rooted in an indigenous educational tradition and the exigencies of a necessarily bi-cultural and social environment.[4] This tension, which was also a keynote of the Haskalah, is perceived as one element in the more general tragedy of Catalan implacement in the dominant Castilian state.

Thus, the second root of Catalan philosemitism, the feeling of attraction to Jews as a people who have collectively suffered by virtue of their ethnicity, is related directly to the recent history of Catalonia. For the Catalans had reconstructed their culture, achieving a level of brilliance comparable even to the great literary flowering of the later middle ages, only to have it threatened with extinction. Most Catalans (of the political left and right alike) supported the Republic in the Civil War (1936-39), during which the protection of their hard-won autonomy became a key rallying point. "Separatism" (inevitably styled "Red separatism"—*rojoseparatismo*—by demagogic opponents of cultural autonomy) was in turn one of the prime bogeys of Franco's "crusade." The Catalans and Valencians held out until the very end of the war, the fall of Barcelona in early 1939 marking the final collapse of the Republican cause.

Franco's victory brought with it an attempt to suppress Catalan culture and to root out all of its overt manifestations. The use of Catalan was barred in the schools, mass media, and even in church. During the dark days that followed, even socialists made the pilgrimmage to Montserrat where the monks openly defied the ban and sermonized in Catalan, thus paving the way for a new regionalist coalition of the church, the bourgeoisie and the democratic left, exemplified in the 1960s by the monthly *Serra d'Or*.

At the height of the repression—1940, 1941, 1942—when Catalans had become cultural exiles in their own land, Barcelona was flooded with Jewish refugees fleeing the Nazis.[5] It was no doubt at this moment that many Catalans became impressed with the similarity of the plight of the two peoples. The impression was a deep and lasting one. In the mid-1960s, one of my classmates from the University of Barcelona assigned a theme to her elementary school class, without prior discussion, on the subject of "The Jewish People." Believing traditional Catholic antisemitism in Spain to be stronger than in fact it was, she was surprised by the results. Of twenty-odd students, only one mentioned the charge of deicide, traditionally prominent in Spanish catechisms. All the rest, without exception, wrote on the suffering of the Jews at the hands of the Nazis. To the Valencian sociologist Lluis Aracil,[6] Catalan philosemitism is a purposeful attitude of identification which plays a crucial role in Catalan nationalist ideology and, as such, throws light on the position of Catalonia within the Spanish state. The Catalan, with good reason, sees himself as a member of a persecuted minority and easily makes the obvious comparison between the Jewish condition in Europe and his own. The forms and products of Castilian *méfiance anticatalane*—for example, the vicious stereotype of the "*perro catalán*" (Catalan dog), as an unscrupulous, traitorous miser—are only too homologous to the products of antisemitism.

Spanish reaction to the Six Day War (1967) revealed overtly the counterpoint between Catalan identification with Israel and Castilian (i.e., the Spanish state's) support for the Arabs. Castilian philoarabism, which is beyond the scope of these notes, is as fascinating and as deeply rooted in popular ideology as is Catalan philosemitism. In Aracil's view, the official Froncoist pro-Arab stance reinforced and partially disguised its antisemitism. These attitudes were crystalized by the Six Day War when strikingly symbolic graffiti slogans appeared on the walls of Barcelona: *Visca Israel!* (Long live Israel!), in Catalan, and *Mueran los judios* (Death to the Jews!), in Castilian. While the Castilian press was generally hostile to Israel, following the government in support for the Arabs, two hundred Catalan intellectuals published a signed manifesto declaring support for Israel in terms best understood in the light of their own nationalist aspirations: "We firmly believe in the right of the Jewish people to possess, re-establish and constitute a State, and we admire their heroic effort of national revival. We despise all attitudes, based on antisemitism, which would attempt the extermination of the Jewish people."

After the Six Day War, a visible breach in Catalan sentiment which had once been nearly unanimously philosemitic and pro-Israel became apparent. *Serra d'Or* records the pro-Palestinian stance of a sector of Catalan intellectuals, typically social scientists who have adopted an anti-imperialist line with regard to Israel.[7] But the philosemitic current persisted too, especially among intellectuals of an artistic or humanistic bent. A somewhat later article described Catalan musical contacts with Israel, in which the author compared the musical situation of Israel with that of greater Barcelona (each area with a population of about three million) in adulatory and even envious terms. Here we see once again the Catalan intellectual's admiration for a small country which had achieved world stature in a cultural field, despite its smallness and isolation. In this sense the author, reflecting upon the impoverished musical scene in Barcelona, refers to the "cultural castration of Catalonia" at the hands, it is implied, of the Castilian authorities.[8]

Mallorcan attitudes towards Jews presents a curious and paradoxical counterpoint to Catalan philosemitism. While Catalans of the mainland have developed an emotional attachment to Jews without benefit of any significant contact with them, those of the island of Mallorca have stigmatized as Jewish a social group—the Chuetas (*xuetes*, in Catalan)—who display no culturally Jewish characteristics at all, and who may not even be Jewish by ancestry.[9]

The Chueta problem began in the late seventeenth century when the residents of the Argentería or Platería (street of the silversmiths), a surviving street of the medieval Jewish quarter of Palma, were rounded up and tried by the Inquisition. As a result of two *autos de fe* in 1675 and 1691 the unfortunate victims had their names written on penitential *sanbenitos* which were then hung in the Cathedral on permanent display. In this manner, the surnames of fifteen families of Palma became stigmatized with Judaism. However, the original list of victims was not an enumeration of *conversos* per se, but simply a census of residents of the Argentería, some of whom, but by no means all, were of Jewish descent. These fifteen family names, in turn, became indelibly associated in the popular mentality with Judaism, the taint of which soon extended to others of the same surnames inhabiting the island. All these names were typically Christian (Forteza, Fuster, Valls, etc.) and Mallorcans with obviously semitic names such as Maimó or Daviu completely escaped persecution. By 1955, the Chueta population of Palma, based on a tabulation of families with the tainted surnames, was reckoned at 5661, or 3.25% of the city's population.

Like Jews in other European countries, Chuetas were consistently shunned, and their relations with people of other social classes could at times be described as normal (especially in business dealings) but never intimate. More a caste than a class, they had their own schools and religious confraternities, did not mix socially with non-Chuetas and entered into endogamous marriages. Segregation was pervasive. The essayist Gaziel used to tell a story about the Mallorcan socialist who failed to see anything peculiar about Chuetas eating by themselves at a political outing.[10] In order to prove their orthodoxy, moreover, the Chuetas have consistently practiced an extremely devout brand of Catholicism and have been noted for public displays of exaggerated piety.

Because of their stigmatization as a pariah group and their consequently marginal position in Mallorcan society, the Chuetas came to emulate in many ways the typical social status of Jewish enclave groups elsewhere. Thus Chuetas are described in stereotypes all too familiar to European Jews: they are said to be skilled in business and avaricious, to have large noses, and to feel inferior to outsiders. They were—and are—in fact mostly businessmen, typically jewelers, and like their Jewish counterparts, tend to be creatively inclined: most piano and violin teachers in Palma today are Chuetas. In the past century many prominent Mallorcan churchmen were Chuetas, in spite of the fact that numerous religious establishments on the island excluded Chuetas by statute, and Chuetas participated vigorously in the Mallorcan contribution to the Renaixença.

A group which everyone agreed to forget (except when the issue of equality arose) the Chuetas have not been dealt with thematically by Mallorcan writers. But lack of frequent mention is to a certain extent compensated for by the quality of the literary productions in which Chuetas do play a role. I refer, in particular, to Llorenç Villalonga's novel, *Mort de dama*.[11] In this sardonic commentary on the traditional values of Mallorcan aristocracy, Villalonga introduces the Chueta theme personified in the character of the poetess Aina Cohen, "daughter of a little silver maker in the street of the Platería." Aina is made to exemplify the conservative, traditionalist and narrowly regional brand of intellectuality associated with the Mallorcan *renaixença*. (Ironically, the Chuetas allied themselves with traditionalist, aristocratic cultural institutions, rather than the liberal groups which would, perhaps, have been more inclined to treat them with a greater semblance of justice.) By this device, and by giving Aina a *Jewish* rather than a Chueta name, Villalonga is able to play upon the her self-hatred and, in my interpretation, make a moral statement about the position of Catalan intellectuals in contemporary Spain: the Catalan intellectual as Jew, the archetypical outsider. Self-hatred is the keynote of Aina's personality:

> She did not understand . . . that in part she had driven herself mad through an impulse which made her humiliate herself unnecessarily before the race which, centuries before, had burned her ancestors. All the Hebrews of Palma were traditionalists and *enragé* Catholics, because Mallorca and the Church

had dealt with them like no one else. More intelligent and cultivated than the median level of the island, almost all well-to-do, it would be difficult to sort out the obscure reasons for such masochism.[12]

In Villalonga's account there is no intent to present a maudlin or even sympathetic view of the Chuetas. (Villalonga was himself a conservative aristocrat.) The tone is sometimes empathetic, but more often mocking or scornful, and the neurotic Aina is not a sympathetic character. But Villalonga was a psychiatrist by profession and his professional insights, cutting and accurate, must perforce transcend his characterization of the poetess to illuminate the social position of the despised class. In *Mort de dama*, the reader senses again the isolation of the Catalan intellectual, made vivid by the implicit comparison with a self-hating and persecuted ethnic minority. Aina's masochism, her transcendent fears, are not so hard to explain, not to a Jew in any case.

Against this background it is understandable that Catalonia's (and perhaps Spain's) leading contemporary poet, Salvador Espriu, should make the parallel trajectories of the histories of the two peoples, Jews and Catalans, the cornerstone of the metaphorical imagery of his poetry. In his play, *Primera història d'Esther* (First Story of Esther, 1948), Espriu articulated in a biblical motif the parallelism between the Catalan and Jewish experiences. By placing the action simultaneously in Sinera, a village of the Catalan coast, and Susa, the capital of the Persian Empire, the poet achieved a dramatic mingling of two myths in a common tragedy of conquered peoples dwelling within a great empire.

Espriu developed this theme in a succession of works constructed with Old Testament and apocryphal imagery: the destruction of the Temple, the dispersion, and finally the symbolic land of settlement, Sepharad. The choice of terms is significant. Just as for the Jew, "Palestine" lacks the charged ideological value of "Israel" so too does the Catalan find "España" wanting as a term expressive of his homeland and national aspirations. (Thus Catalan historians often prefer the term "Hispania," more purely geographical, and lacking in the political and cultural connotations of "España").

More than any other of Espriu's works, however, it was *La pell de brau* which best embodied for me this spiritual symbiosis of Catalan and Jewish sentiment. I felt that in the poet's description of the struggles, anxieties and hopes of Sepharad—that Spain within Spain, a spiritual and mythic homeland—I could also perceive an evocation of a mythic Jewish past with which I could identify intimately.

When the foregoing remarks were first written, in 1972, the public culture of the Franco regime seemed to have been every bit as rigid and timeless as when I had lived in Barcelona in 1960 or in Valencia in 1965. The transition to democracy released a current of cultural change and renovation that rapidly displaced my experiences of the previous decade into a past seemingly more remote than the actual passage of years would indicate. When the Catalans regained their cultural autonomy, philosemitism receded into the cultural background, replaced by symbols more directly related to the politics of national reconstruction. The image of Israel as a beacon of hope was no longer a necessary referent. With the added perspective now of fifteen years it is clear to me that philosemitism was for a repressed generation of Catalans an expression of the survival both of self and of one's own culture in a time of political and linguistic oppression and cultural immobility. To identify with Jews was a form of covert opposition to the regime. In 1965 a friend named Fuster gravely assured me of his Jewish ancestry, since many forced converts in Valencia had taken artisanal surnames in the late fifteenth century. The same year, a colleague named Piñero no less insistently informed me that his own Jewish ancestry was beyond doubt, in view of the fact that in Murcia converts named for trees were typical. Against a regime which adopted Catholic symbols in place of ideology Jewishness was an obvious standard for a progressive intellectual to raise. When in very recent times Spain's socialist government extended diplomatic recognition to Israel it was simply redeeming part of the vision of hope and suffering that sustained democracy in its long years of internal exile.

—Thomas F. Glick

Boston, February 1987

NOTES

1. Thomas F. Glick, "José María Millás Vallicrosa (1897-1970) and the Founding of the History of Science in Spain," *Isis*, 68 (1977), 276-283.

2. *Tirant lo Blanc*, David H. Rosenthal, trans. (New York, 1984).

3. "El renaixement de l'hebreu," Vol. 2, no 9 (Sept. 1960), 9-10.

4. On diglossia and related social and cultura problems in contemporary Barcelona, see Francesc Candel, *Els altres catalans* (Barcelona, 1964). For Valencia, Rafael Lluís Ninyoles, *Conflicte lingüístic valencià* (Valencia, 1970).

5. See Haim Avni, *Spain, the Jews and Franco* (Philadelphia, 1982), *passim*.

6. Personal communication.

7. See Jordi Solé-Tura's characterization of Israel as an imperialist power in *Serra d'Or*, 9 (1967), 706. A full-fledged pro-Palestinian stance is that of Joseph M. Gonzàlez Ruiz, "Per una pau justa a Palestina," *ibid.*, 12 (1970), 396-398. But see Eduard Feliu's pro-Jewish reply in the same vol., pp. 927-928 and Gonzàlez Ruiz's defensive rebuttal, "No som antisemites," *ibid.*, 13 (1971), 99.

8. Guillem-Jordi Graells, "Contactes amb Israel," *Serra d'Or*, 13 (1971), 599-600.

9. On the history and sociology of the Chuetas, see two important memoirs by Chuetas: Miquel Forteza, *Els descendents dels jueus conversos de Mallorca: Quatre mots de la veritat*, 2nd ed. (Palma de Mallorca, 1970); Gabriel Cortès Cortès, *Historia de los judíos mallorquines y de sus descendientes cristianos* (2 vols., Palma, 1985) and my review of the former in *Jewish Social Studies*, 33 (1971), 230-232; Baruch Braunstein, *The Chuetas of Mallorca* (Scottsdale, Pa., 1936; reprint ed., New York, 1972); Francesc Riera, *Lluites antixuetes en el segle XVIII* (Palma, 1973), and my review in *Jewish Social Studies*, 36 (1974), 307-308; Kenneth Moore, *Those of the Street: The Catholic-Jews of Mallorca* (Notre Dame, 1976), and my review in *Jewish Social Studies*, 40 (1978), 323-324; and Dan Ross, *Acts of Faith* (New York, 1982), chapter 3.

10. Forteza, *Descendents*, p. 100.

11. First published in 1931; I have used the sixth edition (Barcelona, 1967). Three editions have important prefaces: the first by Gabriel Alomar; the third (1954) by Salvador Espriu; and the fourth (1965) by Joan Sales, reprinted in the sixth. See also Villalonga's discussion of Forteza, "Un comentari a un llibre de Miquel Forteza," *Serra d'Or*, 9 (1967), 401-402.

12. *Mort de dama*, p. 98 (my translation).